T0308604

FICTION

CONOR O'CALLAGHAN

FICTION

Wake Forest University Press

Wake Forest University Press

Copyright © Conor O'Callaghan
First North American edition published 2005

All rights reserved. For permission to reproduce
these poems in any way, write to:
Wake Forest University Press
Post Office Box 7333
Winston-Salem, NC 27109-7333

Printed in the United States of America
Library of Congress Catalogue Number 2005927658
ISBN (paper) 1-930630-23-9
ISBN (cloth) 1-930630-24-7

First published in Ireland in 2005 by The Gallery Press
(Peter Fallon, Editor)

Contents

'I have given here my own opinions and impressions, and I have no doubt my committee differs from some, but I know no other way of writing. We had all our points of view, though I can only remember one decision that was not unanimous. A member had to be out-voted because he wanted to substitute a harrier for a wolf-hound on the ground that the only occasion known to him when hare and wolf-hound met, the wolf-hound ran away. I am sorry that our meetings have come to an end, for we learned to like each other well.'

— W B Yeats, 'The designing of Ireland's coinage',
The Coinage of Saorstát Éireann 1928
(The Controller, Stationery Office, Dublin 4)

for Joan

Coventry

On a night as clear and warm as tonight,
in 1941, a stray German squadron
with a war to win and a radar on the blink
mistook the quays of neutral Seatown
for the lights of greater Coventry.

On a night as clear and warm as tonight —
when she has gone into an almighty huff
and taken the chat over heaven-knows-what
(or something of nothing with a bit of fluff)
and my lot once again is the box-room futon,
the guest duvet —
                    I am inclined to think
perhaps the Luftwaffe after all were spot on,
and would give my eye-teeth for butterfly bombs
to fall into this silence I have been sent to.

Nineteen Eighty-five

The old man goes AWOL for once and for all.
On my bedside table, from one end of the year
to the next, a press clipping of Mengele's skull,
a second-hand copy of *L'Étranger* in translation.

Our maths teacher is a big noise in CND.
Somewhere between Easter and the post-exam hoolie
the local paper snaps him in his fallout shelter,
the first of its kind in the twenty-six counties.

There follows a summer of drizzle to break records,
of coaches daily from the square to Ballinspittle,
of leaflets explaining procedure in a four-minute warning,
of believing the nuclear winter can be sat out

with back issues of *Reader's Digest* and curried beans,
of afternoons rewinding through *When the Wind Blows*
on a video recorder the size of a dialysis machine
at a time when nobody wonders if it might never.

And little else. Jimmy Hill blubs over Heysel.
Rock Hudson kicks the bucket. September is unsettled.
Mexico City sifts for what's left of itself in rubble.
I make the first of several bids for freedom.

A bit like the wheaten pup a couple of doors down
that chases shadows across the field of a new estate
and isn't seen again despite its owner's weeks of hope
and the ads in shops about it answering to 'Gorbachev'.

There I am — sixteen or so, going on eleven —
thinking myself the last word in a navy Crombie
fetched from the wardrobe of the middle bedroom,
a PLO scarf, a Flock of Seagulls haircut;

smitten with the romance of an umpteenth bomb
on the line in as many days, with my new-found
existential solitude borne of having nobody
— *nobody* — on the platform to wave me off.

Lovelife — The First Flush

The buzz of staying up for Easter in the flat
fades like a question unanswered three gardens over,
the postcard of *Déjeuner sur l'herbe* on the freezer,

next door playing Korngold lieder at full blast,
the partition wall banging, the landlord's lawnmower,
a train braking, the payphone ringing out upstairs.

Gloves

Making out with you
with the lights up full
might as well feel
like thinking
about the dark
inside of gloves.
I love that,
the lining unravelled,
your fingers' smell.
I even learn to love
the fluorescent strip
stammering to life,
the fact that fucking
might as well be
the only way we have
of looking down the barrel
at the gaps in the cold.
Then you take off,
and snow might as well fall
for years on end,
and yours are still
knotted or rolled
on the dumbwaiter
on the landing —
even after all
the bulbs have blown
and you've tried on
that excuse to return
once too often
and the room
has changed hands —
the left pushing the right
inside out.

Out-takes

Somewhere for anyone to happen on,
unheard, unreferenced, on master tape,
my out-takes, their edges of completion,
still survive as leftovers from a cleaned up
final version. They have been filed away
for someone killing time in an archive
to stumble across while his fiancée
collects her coat and pay cheque and clocks off:
my nervous coughing; a few pat words
of instruction; the dry run that amounts
to attempting 'Baa Baa Black Sheep' backwards;
fingers drubbing; some seating adjustments;
the technical hitch purring like a fridge
in the wee hours; an entry off cue;
a pitcher of tap water clinked; the bridge
of 'Norwegian Wood' lilted out of key;
a gag about old dentures that falls flat
after tripping on *grasps*, slurring the same
diphthong twice; groaned from the editing suite —
'And from the top again in your own time';
a pause to wangle a cut for the news;
the reel let run through apologetic
yawns and ill-judged ad-libs and the tannoy's
pointers on pronunciation; static
like rain on a skylight; a clearing throat;
the suggestion of five to download
three seconds of wind through a field of wheat
or footsteps approaching on an asphalt road;
blowing on coffee with neither sugar
nor milk; a last pre-emptory sniffle
within range; the odd expletive on air;
a hangover's residual crackle
swept beneath the first riffs of a fugue;
requests for a breather and a script rethink;

stammering on flashbacks of last night's fug;
a Swatch bleating six; mid-sentence, a blank
or fluff or coming too close to the mic
at the thought of underthings on a floor;
a door sighing shut; my mumbling junk like —
'I'm not sure I can do this any more.'

Formal

The weekend shuttle to the mall at King of Prussia, every hour on the hour from Main Lot past the light-rail line and gratis on the college. We disembark one evening into Seniors trussed up for their end-of-year formal. We're just arriving back and they're waiting to depart — bare arms, shifts, rented tuxedoes, roses — like revenants of a garden party between the wars. We separate, we drift between them, elvers scattered by the slightest current. We're ancient, alien, transparent, retiring further from the same young night they're still graduating towards, its consent of age, its coming. They can't see us and we, much as we want to, can't make them. The driver bounces the embers of his Marlboro into magnolia petals, yawns 'All aboard' in a mock-southern accent. The bus slips off down Lancaster in the direction of the interstate, leaving the parking lot deserted but for us, and even we (what's new?) are scarcely here.

The Count

There's this pal of a pal who earned his stripes
snipping surplus nipples from made-for-TV flicks.
As little as six or seven frames apiece,
they curled in a box at his feet like locks of hair
or like shavings planed from a strip of maple.

Me? I like to think I get my kicks elsewhere.
Still, his nickname lingers on the tip of my tongue
whenever I lose all hope of something worth seeing
and hit the standby through a late double bill,
or whenever I cut my teeth on a sweet red apple.

Reception

Take this whatever way you will, and you will.
Earlier, when I stepped into my name being called,
the applause like hailstones on a felt roof,
the lull, my pre-rehearsed banal 'Nice to be here',
I couldn't help wonder if you or some sad sap,
twiddling the tuner while a future dawn was breaking,
would pick me up in the drumbeats between stations.
Which made me think, swaying through the motions,
of a world visible to my dad from the chimney,
rotating the aerial inches and hanging on the word
— *No* — my brothers and me relayed back and forth
like a bucket of water splashed from hand to hand
to a barn gone up in smoke.

                            I tell a lie.
I overheard that over a glass of ropey Chianti
told by a bloke with a lisp the size of a pup
at the function of the wedding of your cousin,
and remembered the yarn so vividly and often
I took it to heart as part of my own past.
Who am I telling? You suffered it daily
in that hole where we were broke and green as barley.
The heat made Wimbledon a game of join-the-dots.
I'd sit there droning on about the Montreal Olympics,
my pissed father and the mysteries of a picture
that you and you alone could coax around.

Patron saint of sound and vision interference!
Uncrowned queen of tracking and rabbits' ears!
Indulge me while I fill, if just this once,
the singular cup of corn that sentiment permits me.
What I would and wouldn't give to have you with me,
here and now, though closer to what we were,

beside ourselves (no less) with love's indifference,
that you might clarify how this finds me, nicely,
in the aftermath of thank-yous like a wake,
waiting in a three-star lobby on my lonesome
(so help me) to saunter any moment out to the cab
the Japanese brunette on the desk has called me
and the even greater unknown (for heaven's sake)
of tonight's canopy of satellites and nip in the air
a dope such as I can only hope to welcome.

Shanty

The ditty from home
where a low sound greys
in heat like barcode   and sky
recedes beneath its fold
I flicked across three provinces
inland of any shore
and have since turned back on
with chorus enough to keep
the memory of a squeezebox company
and aerials like dandelion seed   from the mouth
of one crossing to many
and many ends hummed
where verses thunder scattered would have fallen

so long

the phrases don't recall if they are
warm or half
measures become a whole
new frequency: the carriage lights of an island
stopped in black or a swell
between passing cars
there   and there again
the air as yet unsung.

Inland

'This is the sea, then, this great abeyance.'
— Sylvia Plath, 'Berck-Plage'

Up here
the air is chaste, literal,
and thirst a one-eyed Jack.
A pick-up stalled on the right-of-way
is squeezing 'So Long, Marianne'
through a whole afternoon's glare.
Lake members drop by with ballgame stats
already sleeved in dust by the time they reach us.

Above all I acquiesce, eat frozen plaice,
praise freshwater's inertia, sit last on the porch.

A couple of bullfrogs court one another with oblique
alternate drags on a flugelhorn and little blocks
of light go down like dominoes on the opposite bank.

Some knowledge
                              you dream, is felt first
ages before it's known. Take dawn, the way it floods
our curtainless room. Drifting out and in

its wake: petrels, white caps, the tide rolled back to Wales,

a lopsided yawl run dry on the unseeded slope
of the lawn by breakfast. I wish.

Time Zones

I drift on an ocean of eucalyptus.
An airbus, forty thousand feet up,
undoes the stratosphere's zip
and darkness opens out between us.

Sleeplessness. Homebirds in another room
are whimpering for me to call back across
an eight-hour lapse, the dawn chorus,
the landing I couldn't be further from.

We bring our long-distance silences to an end
(like Saint Brendan and Saint Patrick
arguing the toss mid-Atlantic),
still none the wiser where we stand.

By now you have long since tired
of the day I'm still midway through.
I can all but feel you ravelling the throw,
minutely, into your half of the world.

Through *Saturday Night and Sunday Morning,*
a late show, I blank out into the internal flight
that makes a straight line of the lights
of Baffin Island and the Black Mountains.

✈

Standing here banging quarters into white space,
feeling like the next turn up on stage,
leaving message after disconsolate message,
sick of the sound of my own voice.

✈

For the time being, being without yours
is being in love with this groundless
momentary displacement of hotel lounges,
a sweater folded around my shoulders.

✈

Mostly, when sleep is beneath me,
I fall all over again for your absence,
the memory of your sap like absinthe's
aftertaste, your scent *this* near to me.

✈

An afternoon in the 80s and it goes black
just like that, the way you envelop
yourself in your crushed velvet wrap.
I head back alone along the beaten track.

✈

I guess I imagine you most while the elevator
is sighing through the motions back to earth
and I'm about to pass up, for what it's worth,
the lobby's foliage for the cold night air.

✈

Time out with seconds to go for the Lakers
is suddenly a film of *The Tin Drum*.
In between, in fits and waves, the dream
of postcards arriving in my wake like echoes.

An hour to boarding, not expecting to, I get you.
The kids have gone down. You've just taken
your flipflops into our west-facing garden
when the phone starts warbling out of the blue.

A biplane from the direction of Idaho
falls past the vanishing point across town
towards the very second it touches down,
a dragonfly landing on its own shadow.

For weeks there we come together
either side of the breakfast cereals:
you stepping out at Arrivals,
me still stuck in Departures.

Once Removed

Making time in the rushlight around dawn
to shake some hands and turn straight back again,

a sniffle of provincial towns, crossroads unsignposted,
standing alone more often than not unbreakfasted

through readings, gifts, the local dog-collar
mumbling up there in the distance behind a pillar

the request for a moment of silent prayer,
and closing my eyes and getting nowhere

or only as far as somehow remembering the bloke
who built our own house, brick by silent brick,

the way his wife and himself would never forget
the first holiday in a B&B in Newmarket

when putting a bit aside was anything but simple,
abroad unheard of, his daughters still small:

their faces in a row at the table, all pigtails
and homemade dresses; good as gold; angels.

The Flat Earth

for Eve

Tilt the garden up and, look, nothing
falls off. A smock leaning through
the window of the dining room
even offers its pattern on a plate.

The surface, love, is everything.
It is plenty. The wallpaper ripens,
the horizon plumbs its own depths
and the flat earth warms to us.

They say they speak apples there,
a patois of wafer and chequered cloth,
the glow a carafe of still water
both gathers and gives back.

It waits for you. Go to it. You're as
full and round as it is and it is all yours.

A Truck of Lemons

An artic of unwaxed lemons, tarp scrolled up to its cabin,
leaves my rent-a-wreck Dodge for dead on an ocean climb.
All evening the local public FM has saturated a graveyard slot

with station identifications, the updated bushfire figures.
Now a truck is shedding enough of its surplus lemons
that the road becomes a mash of softened tar and pulp,

the traffic spaces out and everyone forsakes the air conditioning
to drop our windows and yip like freshmen at a rodeo.
It's innocent, disarming, a rush of colour nailed to its own mast,

landing from every angle into the gulf between charred earth
all around and commuters flagged into one crude stream,
each yeehaw like the refrain of some slackers' credo,

each lemon a chrysalis or votive flame casting flesh and us
when the truck is exited through a number in the distance,
is survived only by the draft of lemons' primary odour

our hoods and lamps go on processing into Pacific dark.
We are blameless. We are yellow. But present us, Sir,
the slipstream of a truck of lemons and you'll find us plenty willing.

The Burbs

Da poco sul corso è passato a volo un messo infernale.

Campus is a morgue. Our sticks and stones are being shipped home
surface, piecemeal, with our accents. The stadium behind gets hired out formally
for high school graduations. We sleep by floodlight's chrome,
dream books in spirit boxes ploughing the Atlantic and salute each family

shortcutting across our yard mid-morning. Our daughter's
karate master's second cousin has been beheaded in cyberspace.
That Saturday kicks off with the mantra: 'Winners never quit, quitters
never win.' Two nights the networks carried the last footage of his face.

Now *nada*. The cicadas are a riot. A kid punctuates the weekend darks
with roman candles and the neighbours believe Armageddon is upon us.
Even the chaplain (christened 'Charlie' by the Ethics card sharks)
reports for duty with beeper swinging from one of his breast pockets

like the buttonhole of a dandy. We live in central air and shades,
skittish with heat, the release of feeling neither here nor there
between several *raisons d'être* and the breezy self each impersonates,
blasting 'The Wind that Shakes the Barley' to smother

another gospel *a cappella* 'Star-Spangled Banner' climaxing on the PA
and blurting all of the above over takeout salad at Mort and Barb's.
The eldest by his first wife is some big cheese in Columbia
with problem teeth. Barb has defected to admin. 'Textbook Burbs',

Mort's prognosis, turns out to be a hobby horse
he saddles up there and then and drones off into the sunset on.
We listen. We embrace the valedictory pause
on the porch where a simple handclasp in the past has done

and avoid them the remains of July and the whole of August.
School falls in the same week the toe-tag figure enters four digits;
my heart hammers to the siren song of a paddy wagon on the interstate
and the fine spell that began Memorial Day unravels in Ivan's outer limits.

A copse of bamboo between the Persians and us clacks like flipflops
so much we pull the screen door shut to catch the update
and I have used a softball nesting in its mitt as ballast to stop
a flotilla of trial assignments on 'The Dead'

from blowing off. One is by the sophomore who sits our offspring.
Generally, she's dropped by her mom in a bumper-stickered Plymouth
and goes clubbing when we get back. Last night I murmured something
like 'Sweet life!' in her wake and pitched that softball into the undergrowth.

The papers, graded red in my hand, peeled off slowly, sheet by sheet,
then caught altogether like fanned flames or a current of doves let go
and come back to earth as ash. This morning they're nowhere in sight.
In the elevator, softly falling through its shaft from class, I eavesdrop 'snow'.

The Middle Ground

We wear this weather the tennis shirts
we once thought a scream. We compromise
when it comes to cuisine and the arts.
We find birth moving. We vote for peace.
We praise long stretches and hire a strimmer.
We call our doctor by his Christian name.
We flick through catalogues in bed. In summer,
we intend to watch less telly, join a gym.

We save up our statutory days of leave
like pesetas in a jar. We place our trust
in the laws of averages and nature. We love
our tots in ways our parents were against.
We do jobs around the house, and see to it
the sitter doesn't walk home on her own,
and phone out for a pizza on Friday night,
and blow every other New Year on the sun.

Our sisters aren't grannies when they're thirty.
Our daughters don't stand in nite-club queues
using language, smoking, looking tarty,
in their teens and gangs and platform shoes.
We don't blare car horns at all hours,
or leave beer cans and cigarette butts
on the pavement. We don't piss in doors.
We don't blame others, or fuck like rabbits.

We wake instead to Sunday's civic order,
still together, to heaven in a garden centre,
an agnostic grace, a roast, and getting older,
milder, lying out the back on plastic furniture.
When the golden hour throws in '80s hits
we hated then, we know the words, we reminisce.
We don't mind if the ground that separates
the high-rises and the horsey set is ours, this.

Crush

MOON

It rises, nameless and requited, from the feather of a goose
in grass to the anglepoise's reflection in the window
still shining after its switch has been pushed to O.
It fills. It thins to whole nights of distraction. It goes.

A black canvas — when one of us never musters 'I love you'
until the other leaves the room (as if the only things we mean
get said in parenthesis and are perpetually marooned between
the last quarter of the old and the first quarter of the new).

SUN

4.16 am, blissed on midsummer, making the most of a brush
with a velvet dress and the scent of dewberry, I keep my secret
secret like someone else's change collected from the cigarette
machine and saved for luck. I am too far gone to sleep. Much.

I sing the praises of the strip lights' glimmer, the twittering land,
the microwave. In kimono, slippers, I set the dial on the timer
and wait as long as it takes. I stand before the sliding door,
hiding a mandarin behind my back. I ask the day, 'Which hand?'

Heartland

It's still going,
    the post-tea siesta
in the towns, and much later than planned,
    when I say my so longs
    and get away
into that antiquated heartland
    full of huckster shops
    and halls and the warmth
with which midsummer flatters itself.
    I make shapes,
        corkscrewing north
and fiddling now and then with the sunroof.

After nine, ten,
    it's still good and bright.
So I pull over in Durrow
    for a pee, a cone,
        give the legs a bit
of a stretch and come around somehow
    to bluffing a bum
    with a plastered hand
about the Land Leagues and the famine
    in a hotel ballroom
        where a two-piece band
is programming its drum machine.

Outside, on the green,
    as if from a shipwreck,
five Spaniards in a hired Toyota
    have settled on
        hitting West Cork
before the day's done. I run the motor,
    flick on the lights.

What darkness follows
is just the Irish underwater darkness
  of horse chestnuts,
      handball alleys
and burger joints with hanging baskets.

  The horizon
      all the way up
goes into one of its purple patches.
  On the roadside grazing
      there are even sheep
marked with aquamarine, and midges,
  with fields of rape
      streaming towards
the dimmers. I pass out and am passed
  by nothing. A tape
      of bluegrass standards
meanders through both sides twice at least.

  The shortened night
      on the long finger,
between Monasterevin and Kildare,
  for a minute,
      or slightly more,
it starts to feel as if its shutter
  won't fall again,
      not properly,
or ever, and I am diving upwards
  through seas of corn
      or maybe barley
and any second now will break the surface.

Fiction

None of this is true.
We're still all
we crack ourselves
out to be.

Our hereafters
have not been laid
in a plot
with my loose ends.

You're not miles away.
The slow numbers
were never
swayed alone to.

I don't blame you,
smiling in the mirror
at a face
you've just made up.

Lovelife — The Middle Years

The penny drops during a fortnight abroad
to an oldest girl who notices her mother
sitting to elevenses and supper in different skirts.

Or to a dust-path in the sticks and an only child,
excused for once from laying the lunch things,
hitting a shuttlecock among cabbage-whites to himself.

Two Removes, Li Po

i

The rectangle of silver
on my bedroom floor
is like an acre of ice
on a January night.

Glancing up through blinds
I see the stadium lights.
Staring down at the boards
I think myself home.

2 TO HIS TWO KIDS

The mulberry leaves are emerald and three times
the silkworms have crashed and come to.
Who, given I won't make this spring either,
will prune the shadows where my family is settled?
Trading the water, there's little I can do.
A southerly balloons my homesick daydream
to the beer garden of our roadside local.
I imagine the peach tree by the east gable
I planted before I pushed off three years ago
with thick leaves, branches rattling, haze blue
and grown as high as the eaves of the roof
while I've been out of the picture. I have you, daughter,
stand beneath it and snap a branch in bloom.
Your tears are still not dammed. I am nowhere.
Little man, already sprouted to her shoulder
and standing out beneath the peach tree too,
nowadays who rubs the down on your neck smooth?
Sense fails me, and daily my heart (I *know*) breaks in two.
I'm tapping out this on a thrift store typewriter
and overnighting it with kisses to you a world upriver.

'Hello'

1 ANTEDILUVIAN

Those were the days
   when Gladstone and Disraeli
were locked on the hustings,
   and the Pianola
was all the rage,
   and Wild Bill Hickok
was outdrawing the gallows,
   and impressions of Mr Longfellow's
The Song of Hiawatha
   were still hot cakes,
and a fellow's cell number
   was a different affair.

Up until that point
   our shipshape antecedents
graded the mornings,
   the afternoons, the evenings
'good' heedless of the day
   in question, the season,
and were kind enough
   to say so, hail or snow,
if only in herringbone tweeds,
   in furs, as a matter
of courtesy or course,
   if only in passing.

2 IT'S FOR YOU

Blame the blower,
since some kind of formula
for an opening exchange
had to be agreed upon
to get the ball rolling.
And not only for the ears
of polite society,
its upper echelons,
but to trip as readily
from the lips of gigolos
and babes and heathens
and saints and regular Joes.
So, think of the host
of suggested possibles
grown yellow around the gills
that were dusted down
and duly given the elbow,
that might just as well
have been Hebrew
to the likes of you and me.
Then, think of the 'hillo'
Hamlet shares
with Horatio,
and you're in the general area.
Think of the huntsmaster,
think of the hounds
and a hare's breath,
and you're there or thereabouts.
Think of the troubadour 'hola',
the Huguenot 'salut',
and you're in the same ballpark.

Think of yola as if barked
by the hoodlums of Hanley,
the zealots of Sacramento,
and you're on the right track.
And think also
of Tristram Shandy's 'Hollo! Ho! —
the whole world's asleep! —
bring out the horses — ',
and you're getting warmer.

3 SCI-FI

There is out there a parallel universe, surely,
where the notional arm-wrestle or dropping coin
landed on the side of another serious hopeful.

Where you and I totter daily through to the hall
to utter the singular and singularly nautical reply,
and every pal is called 'matey' on the mobile,

and the legend for global telecom is Long John Silver,
and Lionel Richie holds the record for weeks at No 1
with a hit loved and sung by sailors the world over.

Where the beautiful and famous and wealthy
fall head-over-heels and age and file for alimony,
weekly, in full colour, in the pages of *AHOY!*

4 AND THE WINNER IS …

The finale
failed to draw
enough hoopla
or more-than-usual hullabaloo
to overshadow,
say, the annual grudge match
of Eton and Harrow.
What would follow
the trawl high and low
as good as amounted
to a classless straw poll
whereby it fell to,
laughably, the hillfolk,
the phoneless hoi polloi,
to swallow a winner.
And the word? Oh, you know…
A brace of syllables,
phatic and simple,
like the mating call
of your average hoopoe,
although originally
aspirated as if with an *ah*
that wasn't just plummy
but ever so.
Imagine inasmuch
as imagination will allow
something as holy
and wholly empty
as any halo,
a halfway house between
a hiccup and a holler,

an alloy
of the heavy-hearted
'halloo, halloo'
Poor Tom howls at the Fool
and an old-fashioned
Honolulu aloha,
a domesticated version
of the hallowed Hallelujah,
only secular and ringing hollow.

5 CAN YOU HOLD?

I give you a bell one night
and there is something about
your here-we-go 'hello',
the first and last we share.

It separates us after that
like an island in my head
where all the lights are out
and all our boats are burned.

6 RETRO

You recognize the drill.
We all do.
A fortnight package
in a hotel on the edge
of half-built Fuengirola
or another similar
heliocentric hellhole
of the south,
and the haul back
via Heathrow
on a bank holiday,
so hungry, so alone,
you blow your credit limit
on a week-old omelette,
your callcard's last hurrah
on buzzing home.
You can hear your phone —
four times, five, six —
its cocktail of yodel
and whooping cough
carrying all the way through
from the choked letterbox
to the kitchen's lean-to.
And, truth to tell,
you secretly can't help
but hope upon hope
it will be picked up
by some other hobo
who isn't you.
Then your own voice,
as though recorded in a portaloo,

desperate to sound human
and wallowing in its echo
like tinned fruit in its juice
or egg yolk in albumen,
answers with the word
that history, old prankster,
has planted in your mouth.

7 HELLO-O …

September and hardly a night isn't given up to
our five year old's school homework and yours truly
and the hapless adventures of Happy and Little Hippo
tipping brand new nouns into their shopping trolley.

We keep tripping on 'broccoli'. I am straight man,
glad to play poker-faced Abbott to her Costello.
She laughs through the gaps in the heavy dad routine,
then has had a bellyful and shapes to get up and go.

Hers is the dismissal, in that lippy sort of way,
so that every ounce of emphasis is weighing on the O.
She knows what she's saying. Was I born yesterday?
Did I come down in the last shower? Hell, no…

8 LANDLINE

'You're breaking up.
I'll call when I arrive.'
So I kill an hour or four,
drowning my sorrows
on *The Long Goodbye*
and checking the dial tone.
I try not to brood
on your cellphone,
the way its secrecy
is like a still-life
bathed in shadow
the blind side of yourself
I have neither will nor code
to see or tap into.
Instead I billow
smoke signals in ribbons
and drifting Os
through the level below
the anglepoise's vigil.
And I know,
I tell myself,
your how-do-you-do?
is humming this way
in big looping lines
over valleys and major roads
and May's shallow night
and the split-second delay,
and any second now
the handset will burst into
its songbird's tremolo
behind closed doors
that I will open,
and I will not let go.

Halogen

Our longest-running gag: I step up to your place,
trip the burglar light and cast myself as Withnail
playing the Dane to camera while you put on your face,
soliloquizing to letterboxes crammed with junk mail.

On a good night, I get about as far as the 'nor' of
... *man delights not me; no, nor women neither...*
when I ham up fluffing my lines or losing my nerve
until the gods begin to stir and the light to splutter.

If it were for real, and that were us, we'd be history
before the programme notes had dried. I'd be toast,
last heard of as the sidekick to an aardvark on kids' TV
or giving classes in transcendental theatre on the coast.

Alas, it isn't. I am here. The time is now. The flat is yours:
your bell, your breath, your prompter's snigger to my 'Yes'.

The Narrator,

during the break in chapter,
gets up to stretch beneath a skylight
and hears seagulls, small girls running.
So many pages since he listened last
that he can't recall how it came to this
or which wall the door was on
or even now what time of year it is.
Are his own pauses, he wants to ask aloud,
out there captivating someone else,
when an absent-minded 'Where was I?'
echoes through and he returns
to the place that you left off.

from *Loose Change*

i 'THE PEACOCK'

We've perfected the disappearing trick.
I'm thinking especially of that old lie
called sentiment and sentiment's rhetoric
that we, together or alone, no longer buy.
Remember reading Carver's 'Feathers' to me,
the one about the meal, the peacock dancing?
When you were done I offered you a penny.
You shut your eyes and said exactly nothing.

ii 'THE HERON'

Dead master. Old posturing taxidermist.
Forgive me when I can't help but hear
my granddad and his like being dismissed.
Or call it, if you prefer, a bookish night too far,
contemplating sonnet after well-made sonnet,
when I think 'Stuff that... *Ignorant men*!
They knew what they knew and acted on it,
as opposed to some folks I could mention.'

v 'THE BULL'

I once hitched a lift in a pick-up
from a senator with a thing for voodoo,
and I once got legless in a china shop
with Lee Harvey Oswald's widow,
and I once left my mark on the divan
of twins who grew up in Daytona,
and I once got through to Bob Dylan
but omitted to push Button A.

x 'THE SALMON'

St Brigid's night, and we lie in separate beds.
All about us the flood-level raises the stakes
above regret's loose change and our heads.
I know, even as I go through whatever it takes
and fuss over the blister on my thumb again,
you're swimming away from me in darkness
where the Castletown crosses into the Creggan
and silver water is given to breaking its banks.

xx 'THE HORSE'

A spin in the roles we've saddled on each other:
the upholder of vision to see the abstract through
and the pleb with a bag of chips on his shoulder.
The last straw is an *assiette Anglaise*. I ask you,
'How would the horseman know to pass by
if not by whoa-ing his nag to a standstill?'
We tour the landmarks of Roquebrune, badly,
stopping off only for Camels and petrol.

l 'THE WOODCOCK'

There are five sides to every story, I'm told.
So let me raise a glass and toast this much,
one last time. Let love come in from the cold,
even if love finds you in someone else's crush
or someone else in yours that's grown too long.
Let us greet the leaf, the blossom and the bole.
Let us praise, together, the harbingers of spring
in your step and your girlish way on the mobile.

c 'THE STAG'

Nineteen hundred and ninety-nine.
I test it between my teeth
when it drops again from the phone.
Take it from me, my sweet,
a high hill is a lonely place.
If only I had the exchange rate
I could begin to pay the price
of screwing my way out of a rut.

Other Titles in This Series

River

My mother has risen
to hunt her bifocals.
The book in my lap
bears an antique street plan
she wishes to read.
While she's gone I run
my thumb along the curve
where a city loses its place
among warehouses,
folded discount stores
and dives called after
the brown water they overlook.
I picture words as tributaries
or the crow's feet
my mother's shut eyes make.
I can hear her downstream
in pitch black on the landing
visualizing aloud a sequence back
to when her borrowed key
steered into our door's lock.

Lovelife — The Home Strait

An olive branch, both given and apologized for
in the same breath. Like the gift of secateurs
that will come to weigh upon the gardening gloves,

freckled with damp, between the French doors
and a row of annuals, until the Grundig runs down,
the day thickens and a lamp in the living room flicks on.

They're Finding Now

that a man needs lies in the back of his head;
that a single bed is an enchanted wood;

that a yacht on the horizon is a symbol of death;
that frocks are best unzipped with teeth;

that a stitch in time saves five at most;
that trips in trains leave women moist;

that every second Australian is christened Wayne;
that aliens prey on parties of one;

that we have reached the end of the line,
of what's yours is yours, mine mine;

that spontaneous combustion is caused by fudge;
that Herman Goering played off scratch;

that Job was known as a bit of a whinger;
that Connemara's Twelve Pins is a ballpark figure;

that love is baloney;
that politics is a last resort of the lonely;

that every great poet must own a cat;
that the Son of God got as jarred as a coot

at the Last Supper
and saved our souls in the midst of a hangover;

that every tragedy ends in tears;
that William Shakespeare has been dead for years,

and Lord Lucan is shacked up with Marilyn Monroe
in a bungalow in the hinterland between Wick and Thurso;

that there's nothing to clarify the meaning of choice
like rattling around an empty house;

that the universe knocks over stars like skittles;
that foghorns are the gods blowing in bottles;

that the human heart will heal much easier
when soaked overnight in a gallon of tequila;

that hopelessness is sold by the yard in hotels;
that the light of day will ring no bells.

They're finding now, at an unearthly hour,
that the marital vows are said for a dare

and meant as a joke
that's lost on the odd sentimental jerk

who swallows it wholesale as if it were gospel
and goes on believing its patter, being gullible,

the last man on the planet the punchline
dawns on, like this, in half-light, alone.

Signing Off

It's just about time to round things up.
Thanks again. That was the sound
of white noise being blown
on a patter that's all for now.

Until next time. After this,
you're on your own. It looks like snow.
Here's a little something to take us
all the way to silence. Wrap up well.

Cover Version

Sugar. Isn't it odd that we've never had a song?
You know, where your pre-history mimes in sync
with mine for three otherwise unremarkable minutes.
It could have something to do with old shared habits
such as learning the lyrics by heart and forgetting the air.
Whatever the reason, it keeps us second-guessing rapture
and wondering in its absence what it sounds like
leaves us dancing to the silence between each track.
So, before we lapse again into mutual self-pity
or succumb to the glamour of being gloomy, permit me.
Since, let's face it, every means is its own end
and every crooner his own one-piece tribute band
and every number a free translation. This, therefore,
goes out to all of those who kick off at the encore
and dispense with the main set, the loner who stays
to watch a lap of honour and ignores the race,
the hopeless case who prefers a rolled gold ring
to eighteen carat, a pale imitation to the real thing.
And goes like this: a remake based on no original
like cloudless blue that yields a minute's rainfall,
a chorus misremembered until it's not the same,
a string of variations on no particular theme.
Imagine 'Always On My Mind' rendered *sean nós*
or a street ballad done as a show-stopper in Vegas.
This is closer to an echo than the crack of a shotgun,
the reconstruction bereft of its night in question.
This is the story that begins with its characters leaving,
a day dawning to the shadows of perpetual evening.
This is the tune they're playing on some station
in the grey light before sunrise that you wake in,
and hold for days and can't quite put a name to.
This is not yet love and yet already love's memento.
This is the arrangement of a standard in its final take

that gets cut after the studio has filled with smoke
and the band splits for home; half-hummed, half-said,
unaccompanied; that surfaces as a throwaway B-side
years from now, ahead of its time and lost in action
like the vivid recollection of something still to happen;
that accentuates the words above the melody, its saccharin,
and how very sad they are, and what they actually mean.

Rightly or Wrongly

I have spread my towel to dry on the bonnet
and yawned through a tome on the Wars of the Roses.

I have forgiven myself my own trespasses
and eaten sweetcorn past its sell-by date.

I have wasted all June in pool-shoes and shades
and taken my turn at skimming duty.

I have renamed us 'The Escape Committee'
and bought the evening air for a song.

I have washed my hands of the day just gone.
I have made my bed, and I am lying on it.

This is Her First Publication

He's already opened it and left it on the table at her name.
It's been so long she'd almost forgotten to expect it.
It's seven-ish, warm, and the shower upstairs is thrumming.

She jumps to the biogs at the back and reads aloud
the sentence of hers she didn't write, on the off-chance
that its sense might prove a little slice of history.

She tries her folks. Her mother's stab at excitement
makes her blush. Her dad will be thrilled to bits
and told to ring the minute he's back from the links.

They cook with only the kitchen's strip lights glowing
and have fun imagining all the people who'll see it.
He says the others seem very samey. Hers stands out.

He says he remembers the clifftop walk it's about.
He remembers the ocean, the moored yachts, the bubbles
blown by kids across their path, like yesterday.

He talks as though the 'you' in the second last line
were him. She changes into her sweat pants, her mules,
and chooses not to wreck the evening explaining.

The phone goes as they're serving. They let it cut out
onto the answering machine. Tomorrow she'll find her dad
asking about copies for his sister, her cousins, in Connecticut.

Then the lapse between dinner and bed, spent in a daze,
her head gone light, the ends of her fingers buzzing.
Even her words on the handful of pages she has

look strange. It's like a feeling of having run through glass
and emerged the other side in a clearing, or being stopped
at a level crossing when there's no sign of any train.

They toast the occasion with cider from champagne flutes,
sprawl on the patio, split a bag of pre-salted pretzels
and watch tonight come out all over in planets.

This is her first publication. She's wrapped in it,
its life happening without her that she'll catch up with.
Inside, the TV is chirping the long-range forecast on Sky.

If this were the city, she tells herself, there'd be sirens,
the dark turning up its volume. Instead there's the silence
they sit in, in a way that makes sitting feel like waiting.

Fall

To unbalance. To keel over, accidentally, or submit to the pressures of gravity.
        To plummet in worth, especially currency.
To lose altitude. To take place at some pre-ordained time and date.
        To swallow tall tales at face value.
To lag such a distance back along the trail as to disappear from view.
        To surrender, especially a country,
to the enemy camped in its margins for all of two nights and three days.
        To vanish from the radar of grace.
To have no qualms anymore when it comes to telling friends and foes alike
        precisely where to stick
their olive branches. To be the kind of sap who lapses now and then
        into clandestine amorous crushes.
To indulge a whole continent its own broadleaf syllable for autumn.
        To arrive back unexpectedly in the afternoon
and happen upon yourself dancing a single-handed two-step on the landing
        to Bechet's 'As-tu le Cafard?'
To go, especially too far. To leave some unknown pal a shot behind the bar
        and teeter out upon the dawn,
its parabola of stars, as wobbly on your pins as any newborn foal.
        To bolt awake on a balcony
and see the horizon's twinset of Med and azure in a Blinky Palermo abstract
        that has lain open in your lap.
To realise the only part of flight you can handle is the moment after take-off
        into a blank of unmarked blue
when you feel like a kite getting nowhere fast or a balloon strung out on helium.
        To listen to sound effect CDs so often
every track eventually returns to a common denominator called 'wind in trees'.
        To think the hymns of Ulrich Swingli funny.
To praise a glass half full of homespun pear brandy that tastes of lighter fuel.
        Also, to dwell on the bruise
of one dropped apple. Also, to descend and keep descending until it becomes
        a sort of *modus vivendi*, a buzz.
Also, to stumble and nonetheless to continue, and always to be happy to go down
        in history as anybody's fool,
and somehow to believe in parachutes, and still to find it within you to forgive
        the leaves whatever it is leaves do.

The Present Writer

answers questions vaguely, as if from a distance;
cares less for the dribs and drabs of his libido;
gets more droll, lachrymose, implicit with age;

has backed from the room, the turntable moving
and a refill pad lying open at the page
with 'swansong' and 'glockenspiel' written on it;

makes collect calls from payphones, lost for words;
has been known to sleep in the rear seat
on the hard shoulder, the hazards ticking;

is given to sudden floods of hope; still dreams
of swimming pools, in sepia; can take or leave
a life in shadow; will whoop out of the blue

and surface on the landing, fork and spoon in hand,
adrift of what the done thing was; doodles butterflies
on the envelopes of unread letters; travels happiest

towards daylight and fancies pigeons; gets a kick
inhabiting the third person, as if talking across himself
or forever clapping his own exits from the wings.

Nomenclature

for Vona Groarke

The exclusive
spoken remnant of Ballymahon Cherokee;
a corncrake's gurgle in August; the better half
of sincerity, spelling out its pronunciation
for the benefit of some dumb phone;
a cork inexplicably

rattling inside
its empty bottle next morning;
the port-wine stain that predates
and survives my shadow's dark; a ride
hitched in a van of Greek origin
yonks ago; a plate

of supermarket rigatoni
picked clean with a tuning fork;
a tail light re-routed through Newark
on account of snow; the family room
of press clippings ring-a-rosied
with vermilion

Bic; a wing-bone
of the poem stork grown
hard and small from wishing and my hip pocket-
's murk; a plot in Tang; a login password
that won't work; the meal spent plastered
within earshot

of a creek;
or, fluttering beneath an Old Glory
fridge magnet, the 'Don't Go Back'
that hailed from a fortune cookie
too sweet to polish off.
I am not myself.

Lately
your given name has gone
without saying, is its own premonition,
and yet brings a loveliness there, an oddity
no less so for being this
ubiquitous

I should gladly take.
I suck the life out of a dozen
Marlboro on the decking behind the house,
file my first under the rest of yours
as if for shelter and resign
myself to dawn's crack.

Ring

It's funny
the way things go.

I go to speak at length
on the length of a lunar cycle

and bite my lip.
It's as if I think

those words for love
I love

are tied on the tip
of someone else's tongue

and think again.
I have learned.

I have learned to mosey
downtown in a hand-me-down suit

when it suits me
and the light shines gold

like the gold of apples
through the shutters of half-shut stores.

I have learned to sing dumb
halfway between

the song of a brass band
a handful of blocks behind me

and the harbour in its finery
until now whenever now comes.

Whenever it comes
to language and the heart

and not meaning to sound phoney
I am in the dark. I mean

I could hold and hold
on some corner

hoping for a start
and start hearing myself breathe

the silence of silent callers.
So tonight for one night only

this caller's pronouncing 'moon'
as if the moon were a freckle

like the freckle on your wedding finger
and my mouth were full of quarters.

This

began with an Oriole pencil I stumbled on among the stalls
of Santa Monica and lost by lunch. It ends thus, and now.
For months there was a play on 'pastures new'
that became a blue sea that changed to something else.

There was something as well about the four walls
of a fortnight or three on the wagon. I'd forgotten also
an image of my gran in her kitchen up until a week ago,
the meadow of butterfly buns, her breathless 'It's very close'.

Then the night before last, after a few maudlin drinks,
I gave myself a table of pals dishing out seconds and thirds
and tippling till the cows come home and leaving the dinner things

for armchairs on the porch and a silence without words
that was nothing of the sort, thanks to this and thanks
to the darkness I threw in, littered with mockingbirds.

Notes

page 30　The epigraph is from Eugenio Montale's 'La primavera hitleriana'; the line, in Jonathan Galassi's translation, reads 'An infernal messenger flew just now along the avenue.'

page 52　The designs for the original coinage of the Irish Free State, featuring engravings of animals by English artist Percy Metcalfe, were commissioned in 1928 by a Senate committee chaired by W B Yeats. At the time of circulation, a columnist with the *Manchester Guardian* wrote: 'The Irish coinage will be acknowledged as the most beautiful in the modern world ... I doubt if any country but Ireland would have had the imagination and freedom to lay down the conditions that would have made such designs possible.' Many remained current after decimalization, becoming obsolete only with the introduction of the Euro in January 2002.

page 70　'It is often suggested that the Irish word *fáinne*, ring, is the origin of the term 'phoney' (originally American slang) based on the practice of selling fake gilt rings to gullible purchasers (cf. E dial. 'fawney', a ring, for which *EDD* gives Ir *fáinne* as the origin), but the connection is not certain.' *A Dictionary of Hiberno-English*, Terence Patrick Dolan (Dublin: Gill & Macmillan, 1999).

Acknowledgements

Acknowledgement is made to the editors of the following where most of these poems, or versions of them, have previously appeared: *Areté, The Bend, The Chicago Review, Dancing with Kitty Stobling* (Lilliput), *De Brakke Hond* (Belgium), *The Dublin Review, The Irish Times, The Journal of Irish Studies* (*IASIL* Japan), *Harper's* ('The Narrator'), *The London Review of Books, Metre, The New Irish Poets* (Bloodaxe), *The New Republic, Poetry* ('Crush', 'This is Her First Publication'), *The Recorder, ROPES, Sunday Miscellany* (RTE), *Times Literary Supplement, TriQuarterly* and *west47.*

'Hello' was originally published as the chapbook, *A History of 'Hello'*, by Grand Phoenix Press in 2003.